Endorsements for the Flourish Bible Study Series

"The brilliant and beautiful mix of sound teaching, helpful charts, lists, sidebars, and appealing graphics—as well as insightful questions that get the reader into the text of Scripture—make these studies that women will want to invest time in and will look back on as time well spent."

Nancy Guthrie, Bible teacher; author, *Even Better than Eden*

"My daughter and I love using Flourish Bible Studies for our morning devotions. Lydia Brownback's faithful probing of biblical texts; insightful questions; invitations to engage in personal applications using additional biblical texts and historical contexts; and commitment to upholding the whole counsel of God as it bears on living life as a godly woman have drawn us closer to the Lord and to his word. Brownback never sidesteps hard questions or hard providences, but neither does she appeal to discourses of victimhood or therapy, which are painfully common in the genre of women's Bible studies. I cannot recommend this series highly enough. My daughter and I look forward to working through this whole series together!"

Rosaria Butterfield, Former Professor of English, Syracuse University; author, *The Gospel Comes with a House Key*

"As a women's ministry leader, I am excited about the development of the Flourish Bible Study series, which will not only prayerfully equip women to increase in biblical literacy but also come alongside them to build a systematic and comprehensive framework to become lifelong students of the word of God. This series provides visually engaging studies with accessible content that will not only strengthen the believer but the church as well."

Karen Hodge, Coordinator of Women's Ministries, Presbyterian Church in America; coauthor, *Transformed*

"Lydia Brownback is an experienced Bible teacher who has dedicated her life to ministry roles that help women (and men) grow in Christ. With a wealth of biblical, historical, and theological content, her Flourish Bible Studies are ideal for groups and individuals that are serious about the in-depth study of the word of God."

Phil and Lisa Ryken, President, Wheaton College; and his wife, Lisa

"If you're looking for rich, accessible, and deeply biblical Bible studies, this series is for you! Lydia Brownback leads her readers through different books of the Bible, providing background information, maps, timelines, and questions that probe the text in order to glean understanding and application. She settles us deeply in the context of a book as she highlights God's unfolding plan of redemption and rescue. You will learn, you will delight in God's word, and you will love our good King Jesus even more."

Courtney Doctor, Coordinator of Women's Initiatives, The Gospel Coalition; author, *From Garden to Glory* and *Steadfast*

"Lydia Brownback's Bible study series provides a faithful guide to book after book. You'll find rich insights into context and good questions to help you study and interpret the Bible. Page by page, the studies point you to respond to each passage and to love our great and gracious God. I will recommend the Flourish series for years to come for those looking for a wise, Christ-centered study that leads toward the goal of being transformed by the word."

Taylor Turkington, Bible teacher; Director, BibleEquipping.org

"Lydia Brownback has a contagious love for the Bible. Not only is she fluent in the best of biblical scholarship in the last generation, but her writing is accessible to the simplest of readers. She has the rare ability of being clear without being reductionistic. I anticipate many women indeed will flourish through her trustworthy guidance in this series."

David Mathis, Senior Teacher and Executive Editor, desiringGod.org; Pastor, Cities Church, Saint Paul, Minnesota; author, *Habits of Grace*

JONAH

Flourish Bible Study Series
By Lydia Brownback

Judges: The Path from Chaos to Kingship

Esther: The Hidden Hand of God

Job: Trusting God When Suffering Comes

Jonah: God's Relentless Grace

Habakkuk: Learning to Live by Faith

Luke: Good News of Great Joy

Ephesians: Growing in Christ

Philippians: Living for Christ

James: Walking in Wisdom

1–2 Peter: Living Hope in a Hard World

FLOURISH
BIBLE STUDY

JONAH

GOD'S RELENTLESS GRACE

LYDIA BROWNBACK

CROSSWAY®
WHEATON, ILLINOIS

Jonah: God's Relentless Grace

Published by Crossway
1300 Crescent Street
Wheaton, Illinois 60187

Cover design: Crystal Courtney

First printing 2023

Printed in China

All emphases in Scripture quotations have been added by the author.

Trade paperback ISBN: 978-1-4335-8326-1

Crossway is a publishing ministry of Good News Publishers.

RRDS 32 31 30 29 28 27 26 25 24 23
15 14 13 12 11 10 9 8 7 6 5 4 3 2 1

With gratitude to God
for
Patti Kopylczak, Heidi Stock, and Maria Trexlar,
and our summer journey through Jonah,
where together we glimpsed the greater Jonah
and the grace that brings us to him.

CONTENTS

THE PLACE OF JONAH IN BIBLICAL HISTORY

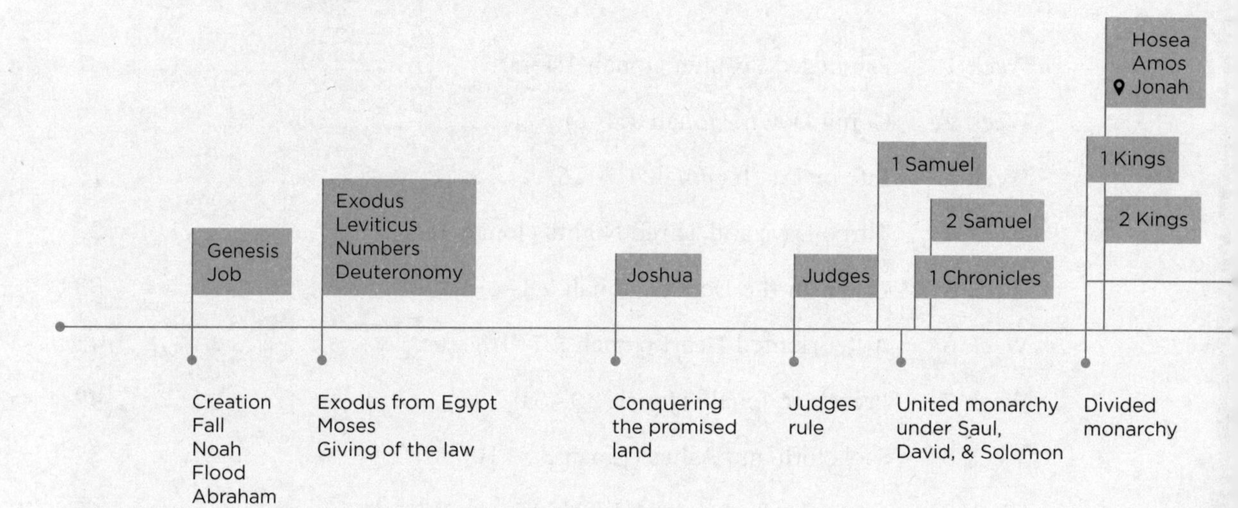

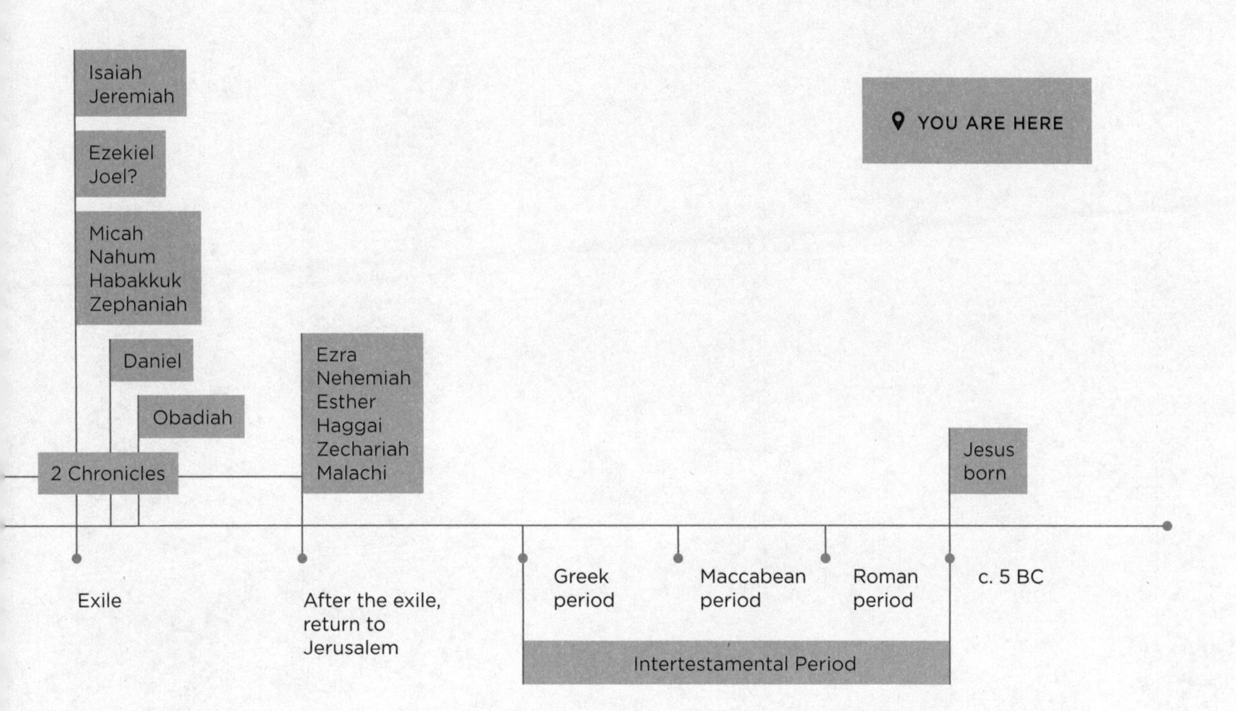

YOU ARE HERE
Isaiah
Jeremiah
Ezekiel
Joel?
Micah
Nahum
Habakkuk
Zephaniah
Daniel
Obadiah
2 Chronicles
Ezra
Nehemiah
Esther
Haggai
Zechariah
Malachi
Jesus born
Exile
After the exile, return to Jerusalem
Greek period
Maccabean period
Roman period
c. 5 BC
Intertestamental Period

INTRODUCTION

GETTING INTO JONAH

Word-association games can be lots of fun and a good way to learn how people think. *Salt . . . pepper. Creepy . . . spiders. Taboo . . . cream-filled donuts. Adam . . . Eve. Jonah . . . whale.* My hope is that this study will remove that last association from your mind forever. If you associate Jonah with a whale, it's likely you learned it during childhood from a Sunday-school felt board. The great fish (not necessarily a whale) is certainly a sensational part of the story, but it's a minor part. The fish is just a bit player in a powerful drama about God's power, wisdom, patience, and relentless grace. The story of Jonah is all about how God works out his purposes and how nothing can thwart his determination to save. We're going to see that the story of Jonah is our story too in our struggles to trust God and submit to his revealed word. Ultimately, we'll see that Jonah's story is really a story about Jesus.

WHO'S WHO IN JONAH

Jonah served as a prophet in Israel from about 760 to 745 BC. He is one of the "writing prophets," which means that he is among those whose prophecies became a book of the Bible. We know little about his life leading up to the events recorded in his book, but we do know from 2 Kings 14 that he had enjoyed a measure of success in his prophetic ministry. Also in the story are the mariners who work on the ship Jonah boards as he runs away from the Lord. There are the Ninevites as well, a people with no knowledge of God until Jonah came along. We must include a few nonhumans in our Who's Who—a great fish, a plant, a worm, and an east wind. Overarching all these figures is the Lord God, who works in and among them to accomplish his purposes.

SETTING

Jonah's story takes place in the mid-eighth century BC. At the time, Israel had fallen far from its glory days under the rules of King David and his son Solomon. In Jonah's day, Israel was no longer a united nation of twelve tribes ruled by one king. The kingdom had divided into a northern

Pronunciation Guide

Amittai: ah-MIT-tie

Jonah: JOE-nah

Joppa: JOP-ah

Nineveh: NIN-ah-va

Tarshish: TAR-shish

portion and a southern portion. Only two of the tribes, Judah and Benjamin, continued to live and worship in Jerusalem in the south, while the other ten tribes lived to the north. Jonah's prophecies were directed to this northern kingdom, which at the time was ruled by King Jeroboam II, one of Israel's many ungodly kings. A bit farther north was the nation of Assyria, a rising empire and ever-present threat to Israel. The Assyrians had a reputation for cruelty, expanding their empire with sheer brute force and subjecting conquered enemies to torture. Nineveh, the city where the Lord calls Jonah to preach, was the military headquarters of Assyria and the center of the empire's violent depravity.

THEMES

We can't help but come away from our study of this book with a deep, awe-inspiring grasp of God's compassion for wayward sinners, for both lost nations and his very own people. Woven in with his compassion is God's mercy and patience. Added together, these attributes showcase God's grace, his pursuit of people who spurn his kindness. God's rule of the whole world—his sovereignty—is visible all through the story, demonstrating how he works through his creation to get people where he wants and to win their hearts. For that reason, repentance is another vital theme. Unbelievers can escape God's judgment when they embrace God and reject sin. And we see the need for God's own people to repent daily of self-centeredness, to prioritize God's purposes and plans ahead of their personal comforts.

The Setting of Jonah, c. 760 BC[1]

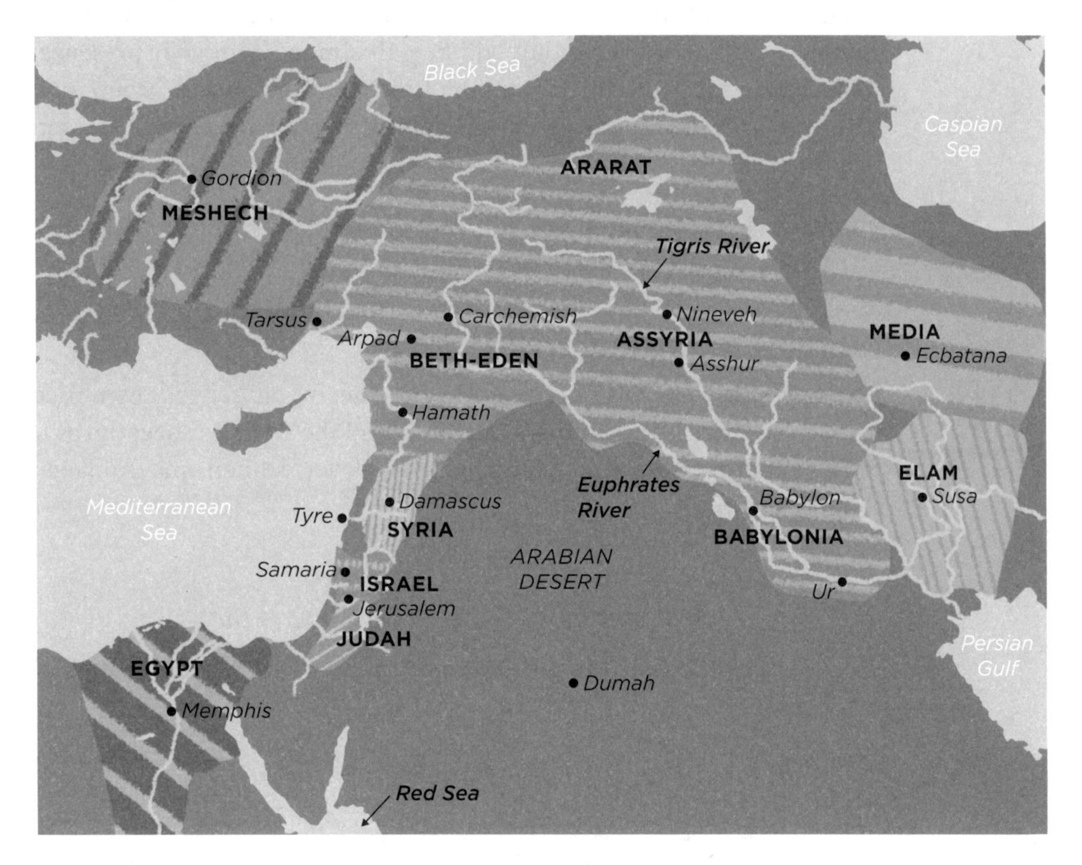

STUDYING JONAH

Although our study of Jonah works through this Bible book verse by verse, you'll benefit from reading through all four chapters before beginning. Since it's a short book, you can read it all in one sitting. Then you can go back and reread each week's portion as you prepare to do the lesson.

GROUP STUDY

If you are doing this study as part of a group, you'll want to finish each week's lesson before the group meeting. You can work your way through the study questions all in one sitting or by doing a little bit each day. And don't be discouraged if you don't have sufficient time to answer every question. Just do as much as you can, knowing that the more you do, the more you'll learn. No matter how much of the study you are able to complete each week, the group will benefit simply from your presence, so don't skip the gathering if you can't finish! That being said, group time will be most rewarding for every participant if you have done the lesson in advance.

If you are leading the group, you can download the free tips sheet at https://www.lydiabrownback.com/flourish-series.

INDIVIDUAL STUDY

The study is designed to run for ten weeks, but you can set your own pace if you're studying solo. And you can download the free tips sheet (https://www.lydiabrownback.com/flourish-series) if you'd like some guidance along the way.

Marinating in the Scripture text is the most important part of any Bible study.

Reading Plan

	Primary Text	Supplemental Reading
Week 1	Jonah 1:1–3	2 Kings 14:23–26; 1 Kings 18:1–46
Week 2	Jonah 1:4–6	Revelation 16:17–21
Week 3	Jonah 1:7–16	Leviticus 16:7–10, 21–22; Acts 27:13–44
Week 4	Jonah 1:17	Matthew 12:38–40
Week 5	Jonah 2:1–6	Psalm 88:6–7; Matthew 27:46
Week 6	Jonah 2:7–9	Proverbs 3:34; Isaiah 44:12–20; Jeremiah 2:11–13
Week 7	Jonah 3:1–5a	Nahum 3:1–7; Romans 2:6–11
Week 8	Jonah 3:5–10	Numbers 23:19; 1 Samuel 15:29; Matthew 12:38–41
Week 9	Jonah 4:1–4	Exodus 34:6–7; Luke 15:11–32
Week 10	Jonah 4:5–11	Matthew 12:39–41

WEEK 1

PRIVILEGED PROPHET

JONAH 1:1-3

Have you ever considered how amazing it is that God reveals himself to people? He certainly doesn't have to. Sometimes we take God's word, the Bible, for granted, don't we? We view our daily Scripture reading as one more thing on the to-do list and even (dare we say it?) as if we're fulfilling a spiritual obligation. That's why it's good to be reminded that the only reason we can know God is that he has chosen to make himself known, first to people like the prophets and later, to us today, through the prophets' message and God's entire written word. Jonah, as one of Israel's prophets, was someone who received God's word straight from the source, from God himself, as we see this week. But on the occasion before us now, Jonah doesn't want to hear God's word, and he does all he can to close his spiritual ears.

1. THE WORD OF THE LORD (1:1)

To Jonah is given one of the best of good gifts:

> "Now the word of the LORD came to Jonah the son of Amittai." (v. 1)

We're told very little about Jonah in this first verse other than his father's name, but we do know a bit about Jonah from his earlier years as a prophet, a time when God made him the bearer of good news for God's people. On that earlier occasion, the military aggression of Assyria had weakened another one of Israel's enemies, Syria, enabling Israel, under the leadership of King Jeroboam II, to regain territory that Syria had taken from them in battle. Jonah had prophesied this Israelite victory.

Read 2 Kings 14:23–26, which recounts this earlier episode in Jonah's life.

- How does this passage in 2 Kings liken King Jeroboam II of Jonah's day to an earlier King Jeroboam (identified here in 2 Kings as the son of Nebat), and what does this likeness reveal about the spiritual state of Israel at this time?

The Old Testament Prophets

"Those who were called to be prophets under the old covenant were appointed to bring the people of Israel special messages from God and to watch over the Israelites to ensure that they kept the terms of their covenant with the Lord. Essentially, the Old Testament prophets were spokesmen for God."[2]

- Why, according to 2 Kings 14:26, did God give this good news to Jonah and then carry it out?

Jonah is identified as "the son of Amittai," which means "son of my faithfulness."[3] The name isn't so much about the faithfulness of Jonah's father or of Jonah himself but about God's faithfulness to Jonah, as we will soon see. The actual meaning of Jonah's name is "dove." What does Hosea 7:11 reveal about the meaning of Jonah's name?

2. GET UP AND GO (1:2)

The word God has for Jonah is detailed and specific:

> "Arise, go to Nineveh, that great city, and call out against it, for their evil has come up before me." (v. 2)

If you recall from the introduction, Nineveh was the military capital of Assyria, the headquarters for its ruthless and aggressive army. Although at the time of Jonah's call the growth of Assyria had stalled somewhat, Assyria was still a feared and powerful force in the ancient world and would become a superpower in another generation.

As a prophet in Israel, Jonah was surely familiar with the military ups and downs involving Assyria. Adding to his knowledge was his proximity to Assyria. Jonah's hometown, Gath-Hepher, was only about 500 miles from this enemy nation, and word about the goings-on in Assyria no doubt trickled into Gath-Hepher on a regular basis. (You might want to take a look at the map on page *xv* and fix in your mind the locations of Israel and Assyria, especially the great city Nineveh.)

There was something else that might have shaped Jonah's thoughts about the Assyrians—a prophecy given to a fellow prophet, Amos, who served in Israel at the same time as Jonah. Amos foretold a day when God would turn the military might of Assyria against Israel, God's very own people, because of Israel's refusal to repent of sin (take a look at Amos 3:11).

In light of that background, it's easy to imagine how Jonah might have felt when he received God's directive. This word from God, contrary to the earlier word he'd received that foretold God's work of grace and mercy in Israel (2 Kings 14:25–26), was for the benefit of people who would gladly do harm to Israel. Go to the Assyrians and warn *them*? This new word was a hard word and an unwelcome one for Jonah.

✦ Jonah wasn't the only prophet in Israel to receive a challenging assignment from the Lord. Before Jonah's time, God sent Elijah the prophet to confront evil head on. In Elijah's case, it was the evil of Israel's very own King Ahab. Read 1 Kings 18:1–46, which recounts one of these confrontations, and answer the following questions on the next page.

- How does Elijah respond when the Lord tells him to go to Ahab?

- How does Elijah address the powerful King Ahab? (See 1 Kings 18:17–18.)

- How does Elijah challenge God's straying people in 1 Kings 18:21?

- How does Elijah demonstrate great faith in 1 Kings 18:22–40 and again in 41–46?

- What do you learn from this story about the God-appointed role of Israel's Old Testament prophets?

- Given how the great prophet Elijah responded to the Lord's instructions, history that Jonah surely knew about, how would we expect Jonah to respond when the Lord calls him?

- Jonah is instructed to go to Nineveh and tell the Ninevite people that the Lord sees what they are doing and calls it "evil" (v. 2). Not knowing the God of Israel, the people of Nineveh most likely viewed their ways and their deeds quite differently, so we'd expect them to respond, "Who cares what Israel's God thinks of us?" The real question, however, isn't what they think of God but what God's thinks of *them*. The fact that God takes notice of these Assyrian people and sends Jonah to tell them—what does this reveal about God himself?

3. ON THE RUN (1:3)

The Lord's instructions were crystal clear. Jonah has been told what to do: "Arise, go . . ." He's been told where to do it: "to Nineveh." God has even given him a reason: "their evil has come up against me." There was only one thing for Jonah to do—get up and go. But that's not what he did:

> "But Jonah rose to flee to Tarshish from the presence of the Lord. He went down to Joppa and found a ship going to Tarshish. So he paid the fare and went down into it, to go with them to Tarshish, away from the presence of the Lord." (v. 3)

✦ What words or ideas are found more than once in verse 3, and what does each repetition communicate to us?

Joppa

"Joppa was 35 miles (56 km) northwest of Jerusalem on the Mediterranean Sea and was a major seaport. Joppa had the only natural harbor in all of Palestine. Though the surrounding reefs made it dangerous for ships to enter the harbor, it was still greatly valued because of its strategic location for trade with the west."[4]

✦ How might Jonah's earlier "success"—his prophecy of military victory (the episode we noted in 2 Kings 14)—have contributed to his present desire to run away from God's call to go preach in enemy territory?

✦ How does Psalm 139:7–12 show us the folly of Jonah's actions?

✦ We always pay a price when we run away from God. How do we see the beginnings of that here in Jonah's flight?

✦ Tarshish, Jonah's intended destination, was likely somewhere along the coast of Spain, although no one is exactly sure of its precise location. A ship departing from Joppa would have sailed west in the Mediterranean Sea—in the exact opposite direction of Nineveh. Tarshish is included in a prophecy made by Isaiah, who foretold how God would one day bless this place and other nations. But at the time of both Isaiah and Jonah, that blessing had not yet come. What is indicated in Isaiah 66:19 about the spiritual state of Tarshish at the time of these prophets, and how might that reveal a bit about why Jonah wanted to flee there?

"When you run away from the Lord you never get to where you are going, and you always pay your own fare. But when you go the Lord's way you always get to where you are going, and he pays the fare."[5]

LET'S TALK

1. Jonah was privileged to hear the word of God firsthand, but we are equally privileged—even more so—because we have his word written down for us. What practical means do you use to work it into your mind and heart? How can a saturation in Scripture guard us from running away like Jonah did? Take a look at Proverbs 4:23, Romans 12:1–2, and Hebrews 4:12.

2. Discuss a time when you were tempted to run away from God (or actually did!), a time when you resisted the clear instructions in his word or the wisest path it indicates. How did it work out for you?

WEEK 2

GOING DOWN!

JONAH 1:4-6

We find Jonah where we left him last week—on a ship heading west toward Tarshish on the Mediterranean Sea. Jonah shouldn't have been on board this boat. In fact, he should have been headed in the exact opposite direction, east, toward Nineveh, where God had called him to go. Jonah is running away from God's call. But it's actually much worse—he's running away from God himself. Rebelling against God is always costly. Jonah got an initial taste of this cost when he had to fork over the fare for the journey. But financial loss was just the beginning. As we'll see, the costs continue to mount. While this is a very sobering reality—for Jonah and anyone who runs away from God—hidden within these costs, these consequences, is God's mercy. We're going to see how the Lord moves heaven and earth (literally!) to restore his wayward people and win their hearts.

1. WIND AND WAVES (1:4)

The very first thing the Bible reveals about God, way back in Genesis 1, is that he created heaven and earth and everything in them. But his creating didn't stop once the universe was set in motion. God's creative work is ongoing. He creates every sunrise, all animals and flowers, and each human being down to the smallest detail. The God who created everything has always controlled every aspect of his creation, and we glimpse this power at work here in verse 4:

> "But the Lord hurled a great wind upon the sea, and there was a mighty tempest on the sea, so that the ship threatened to break up." (v. 4)

- "*But* the Lord . . ." The first word of verse 4, *but*, is important because it links us back to verse 3. What does this linking word reveal about the reason for the storm?

- Storms are fascinating to watch from the safety of indoor shelter. We're awed by flashes of lightning and crashes of thunder and the sight of trees bent low by the wind as dense roiling clouds shroud the landscape in darkness. Storms—each and every one—are designed and sent by our Creator God. Pick two or three (or more) of the following passages and jot down what each reveals about the Lord of storms and his purposes for sending them. Afterward write a summary statement that notes any common themes you discover.

    - Exodus 9:13–29

    - Exodus 19:10–20 with Hebrews 12:18–24

    - Joshua 10:7–11

- Psalm 29:1–4

- Psalm 107:23–32

- Isaiah 30:30–32

- Nahum 1:3

- Revelation 16:17–21

- Summary Statement:

As we return to Jonah, how is the storm impacting his journey?

"A genuine Christian will never succeed in fleeing from God; at a certain point of his own choosing, God is certain to step in, and when he does he will act with pinpoint accuracy."[6]

2. CRISIS MANAGEMENT (1:5)

We meet the mariners now, the men who made their living hauling cargo on this ship. We know nothing about them personally other than their responses to the storm:

> "Then the mariners were afraid, and each cried out to his god. And they hurled the cargo that was in the ship into the sea to lighten it for them. But Jonah had gone down into the inner part of the ship and had lain down and was fast asleep." (v. 5)

This was no small storm. We were just told in verse 4 that the Lord "hurled" the wind upon the waters to bring about "a mighty tempest." The mariners were likely experienced at navigating the ship in all kinds of weather, so the fact that they're afraid points to how powerful this storm was.

Despite their fear, the mariners do all they can to secure the ship. The waves washing over the vessel will weigh it down and gradually submerge it, so to stay afloat, they must lighten the load. They begin with the cargo. Into the sea it goes, and with it all their earnings from the journey. Money becomes meaningless when one's life is at stake. Just as the Lord had hurled the wind onto the sea, the mariners hurl the cargo.

- Divesting the ship of cargo was no fear-based reflex. It's what any knowledgeable mariner would do in a storm, whether afraid or not. But fear is what made each one cry out for divine intervention. How does Romans 1:19–20 reveal why they look beyond themselves for help?

- Jonah's rebellion has brought the mariners into a perilous situation, yet we mustn't suppose they were good men deserving of rescue. How do Psalm 14:1–3 and Romans 3:10–12 help us understand why?

- In those days (and in our day too), people who didn't know the Lord God of Israel worshiped other gods and goddesses, false gods that the Bible calls "idols." What does Isaiah 44:10–20 reveal about idols?

✦ Meanwhile, where is Jonah? Surprisingly, almost impossibly, he's asleep below deck. We're told that he had gone *down* below and had lain *down* for a nap. How does this wording carry forward what we're told about Jonah in verse 3?

The mariners cry out to gods that can't help, while Jonah ignores the only God who can. The fact that the prophet is able to sleep in the storm-tossed ship exposes the depth of his desire to escape not only God but also his conscience and the consequences of his rebellion.

3. WAKE UP, JONAH! (1:6)

The captain of the ship makes his precarious way below deck, and he can hardly believe his eyes when he sees Jonah:

> "So the captain came and said to him, 'What do you mean, you sleeper? Arise, call out to your god! Perhaps the god will give a thought to us, that we may not perish.'" (v. 6)

Each mariner has already cried out to his preferred god for help, and the captain wants Jonah to make a plea to his God as well. Like all idol worshipers, the captain preferred to hedge his bets. If his hometown god failed to provide, maybe another one would come through.

✦ Idol worshipers are the same in every age. Centuries later, in the New Testament, the Gentiles—those not part of God's covenant people—sought blessings from whatever god seemed most ready, willing, and able to provide. How does the apostle Paul refute the lies of idolatry in Acts 17:22–28?

We don't set up gods of rivers and sky and fertility today, but we are just as prone to idol worship as the people in Bible times. Modern idols are things like money, fame, and success. The heart of idol worship in every age is seeking life and blessing in anyone or anything apart from the Lord. There is only one real God, of course, who can actually receive worship and answer prayers.

✦ "Wake up, you sleeper!" exclaims the frantic captain. What an interesting choice of words. In waking Jonah, the captain unknowingly gets underneath Jonah's physical drowsiness, penetrating all the way into his current spiritual condition. Read Isaiah 52:1–2, Ephesians 5:11–14, and Revelation 3:2–3. Although these passages are rooted in different times and situations in the history of God's people, the message to spiritual sleepers is the same in each. What is that message?

✦ Centuries later, in a different storm on a different sea, another prophet—the ultimate prophet, the Lord Jesus—was asleep in a teetering boat. Read Matthew 8:23–27 to answer the following questions.

- In what way is Jesus's sleep different from Jonah's?

- Why is the disciples' reaction to the storm similar to the mariners' reaction in Jonah?

"Are we willing to turn to God's Word for new direction? Are we willing to come to God, confessing our sins and seeking power for new obedience? Our unwillingness will never overrule God's sovereign plans, but by turning anew to the way of the Lord, responding either to gentle nudges in our hearts or to chastening storms in our circumstances, we can find anew the path—the way of the Lord—that is marked by blessing."[7]

LET'S TALK

1. Identify some popular idols of today. How can you know if something or someone has become an idol in your heart? Discuss how Isaiah 44:10–20 guides you not only to recognize an idolatrous temptation but also how to crush it out.

2. It's good every once in a while to examine our hearts to see if we are spiritually asleep. Take stock of your own heart while pondering one or more of the following passages: Romans 13:11–14, Ephesians 5:14–21, and 1 Thessalonians 5:6–8.

WEEK 3

LIFE OR DEATH

JONAH 1:7-16

The storm-tossed cargo ship can't withstand much more battering. As the ship is carried up and over the crest of each new wave, the structure weakens, creaking and groaning and taking on water. Jonah has joined the desperate mariners up on deck, but given his state of mind, it's unlikely that he is making much of an effort to help save lives. Only when the mariners can do no more to shore up the ship do they turn their fear in a spiritual direction. Fear has a tendency to do that. We want to pay attention to how fear is expressed in this portion of the story. We're going to see how the pagan mariners act more godly than Jonah, much to the prophet's shame, and how things turn out for them when the sea quiets down.

1. HE'S THE ONE! (1:7–10)

> "And they said to one another, 'Come, let us cast lots, that we may know on whose account this evil has come upon us.' So they cast lots, and the lot fell on Jonah. Then they said to him, 'Tell us on whose account this evil has come upon us. What is your occupation? And where do you come from? What is your country? And of what people are you?' And he said to them, 'I am a Hebrew, and I fear the Lord, the God of heaven, who made the sea and the dry land.' Then the men were exceedingly afraid and said to him, 'What is this that you have done!' For the men knew that he was fleeing from the presence of the Lord, because he had told them." (vv. 7–10)

Desperate circumstances call for desperate measures, so the mariners seek divine guidance. They don't really care where it comes from—they just know they need the sort of help that transcends human capabilities. So they cast lots. No one is quite sure what these lots consisted of in ancient times, but most likely they were some sort of dice or multicolored stones. The Israelites practiced lot-casting as well, looking to the Lord for guidance, and he chose to work through those means to guide his people.

- The lot has fallen on Jonah, and he doesn't try to deny that he's the one responsible for putting them all in this life-threatening situation. According to verse 9, what specifics did Jonah tell them?

- Which of the mariners' questions from verse 8 does Jonah *not* answer?

- How does Jonah's description of himself contradict his life at this point?

What in Jonah's description of God provokes even more fear in the mariners?

2. A FUTILE FIGHT (1:11-13)

> "Then they said to him, 'What shall we do to you, that the sea may quiet down for us?' For the sea grew more and more tempestuous. He said to them, 'Pick me up and hurl me into the sea; then the sea will quiet down for you, for I know it is because of me that this great tempest has come upon you.' Nevertheless, the men rowed hard to get back to dry land, but they could not, for the sea grew more and more tempestuous against them." (vv. 11–13)

Oh, the irony! Jonah, the only one among them who knows the way to life, seems apathetic about life—his shipmates' and his own—while the pagan mariners, who don't know God, are doing all they can to save everyone onboard.

Why do you think that the mariners ask Jonah for the solution to the problem they now know *he* has caused?

Jonah knows what they have to do, and he tells them in no uncertain terms: "Pick me up and hurl me into the sea" (v. 12). We aren't told what motivated Jonah to offer up his life so freely. Does he have a death wish? It seems that, yes, he would rather drown than go to Nineveh with the Lord's message. And we see this very thing later in the story, in the beginning of Jonah 4 (vv. 2–4) when he verbalizes a preference for death over accepting God's way.

We can't know what was going through Jonah's mind right then, but his acknowledging that his death would calm the storm points forward to the eternal calming of a much greater storm—the tempest of God's wrath.

What Jonah does here reflects the scapegoat on Israel's Day of Atonement. On the one day each year when the sin of Israel was dealt with, God ordained that the high priest would come to the tabernacle with two live goats. One of the goats, chosen by lot, would be sacrificed for sin; the other goat—the scapegoat—was sent away into the wilderness (Leviticus 16:7–10). Jonah does something similar to save the mariners. Just as Aaron (the first high priest for Israel) laid his hands on the scapegoat, placing Israel's sins on its head, and sent it away into the distant wilderness (Leviticus 16:21–22), so also Jonah removed God's wrath by taking his sin into the wilderness of the deep.[8]

"This story is in reality the precise intimation of an infinitely vaster story and one which concerns us directly. What Jonah could not do, but his attitude announces, is done by Jesus Christ. . . . It is solely because of the sacrifice of Jesus Christ that the sacrifice of Jonah avails and saves."[9]

Instructions for how Israel was to observe the Day of Atonement were given in Leviticus, a book of the Bible that sets out the ways God's people were to deal with their sin and impurity in order to dwell with a holy God.[10] Centuries later, the New Testament book of Hebrews reflects on this Day of Atonement and explains why its ritual—a scapegoat—is no longer necessary. How does Hebrews 9:7–14 reveal the way in which Jonah's declaration in 1:12—"Pick me up and hurl me into the sea; then the sea will quiet down for you, for I know it is because of me that this great tempest has come upon you"—is a forward-pointing sign?

✦ The mariners do all they can to avoid doing what Jonah has guided, working furiously to preserve every life on board. In what way does the Lord reveal himself to the mariners in verse 13?

3. THE LORD REIGNS (1:14-16)

The mariners' efforts aren't working. The harder they row, the stronger the storm grows. The moment comes when they realize that they can do nothing to save their lives.

> "Therefore they called out to the LORD, 'O LORD, let us not perish for this man's life, and lay not on us innocent blood, for you, O LORD, have done as it pleased you.' So they picked up Jonah and hurled him into the sea, and the sea ceased from its raging. Then the men feared the LORD exceedingly, and they offered a sacrifice to the LORD and made vows." (vv. 14–16)

✦ What clues do we have in verses 14–16 that the mariners' appeal to the Lord arose from genuine faith and not just fear?

✦ How do verses 14–16 reveal the way God sometimes works to bring forth faith?

✦ The book of Acts records a time when the apostle Paul and his missionary companions were traveling by ship along the coast of Crete. Because it was winter, the season for especially rough seas, Paul had advised against setting out on the journey, but the ship's captain wanted to press ahead, so the band of men along with a large contingent of mariners and prisoners set out. As Paul had cautioned, a strong storm kicked up and soon jeopardized the lives of everyone on board. Read about this incident in Acts 27:13–44. How does this incident at sea stand in contrast to the one in Jonah, and what makes it different?

> *"God will save whomever he desires, whether we are faithful and obedient or not. Jonah's willingness to witness to the Gentiles did not determine God's will for their salvation; all it determined was whether or not Jonah would be blessed by it."*[11]

LET'S TALK

1. How grievous when the world acts more godly than Christians! Describe a time when you've witnessed this or been guilty of doing it yourself. We learn from Jonah's story that even the failure of believers cannot alter God's plans to save, though such failures do mar the beauty of our Christian witness. In what area of your own life are you prone to either marring or hiding the light of the gospel? What practical steps can you take to restore the light to your words and ways in those areas?

2. Jonah claimed to fear the Lord, meaning that he worshiped and served God. His actions contradict his claim, however, so what he really feared was serving his God. We're told that the mariners feared also, but theirs was a different type—they were "exceedingly afraid" because of the storm. Talk about how you have experienced both godly fear—the fear of the Lord—and the mariners' type of fear. How is the terror the mariners experienced remedied by true fear of the Lord?

WEEK 4

THREE DAYS AND THREE NIGHTS

JONAH 1:17

When we left Jonah last week, he'd been tossed into the sea by frightened mariners. As soon as Jonah hit the water, the winds quieted down and the seas calmed. The mariners recognized that Jonah had spoken accurately—the Lord God of Israel had caused the mighty tempest because Jonah was running away. The miraculous end of the storm opened their heart-eyes to believe in the one true God, and they worshiped him. But where was Jonah? We'd expect that he'd have quickly drowned, driven down, down, down by the relentless breaking waves. But that's not what happened. The same God who sent the life-quenching storm sent a life-saving miracle into its depths. We're going to focus on that miracle this week, which we find all in one verse—arguably the most important verse in the entire book. We'll see how the Creator God worked in and through his creation to save Jonah's life, but even more important is what this work points to—another life-saving miracle that would come centuries later.

1. A GREAT FISH (1:17)

The Lord who had hurled the wind upon the sea to stir up a mighty storm, and then stilled that very same storm, now directs another part of his creation to accomplish his purposes:

> "And the LORD appointed a great fish to swallow up Jonah. And Jonah was in the belly of the fish three days and three nights." (v. 17)

Did this really happen? Many people see this episode as nothing more than an exciting Bible tale to teach in children's Sunday school. "It's not possible," they reason. "No one could survive all that time inside a fish. No doubt they've missed the reports of scientific evidence to the contrary. More importantly, those who doubt aren't taking into account that the Creator God can do as he likes with humans and fish and everything he's made. To that end, perhaps this was a special one-time-only miraculous fish with the capacity to host a live human. But what most solidifies this incident as true history are the words of Jesus himself, who, as we will soon see, speaks of Jonah's time in the fish as a real event.

- Before we look at the specifics of this verse in Jonah, read through Psalm 104 and note what you see there about God's intentions in, through, and for his creation.

Expiation and Propitiation

"*Expiation* is the act that results in the change of God's disposition toward us. It is what Christ did on the cross, and the result of Christ's work of expiation is *propitiation*—God's anger is turned away. The distinction is the same as that between the ransom that is paid and the attitude of the one who receives the ransom. Together, expiation and propitiation constitute an act of placation. Christ did His work on the cross to placate the wrath of God."[12]

2. DOWN UNDER (1:17)

The primary setting to this point in the story has been the sea. Water holds great significance in the Bible. The Lord uses seas and rivers and even man-made wells to reveal himself and his ways to people.

- What do we learn about God from the water in each of the following passages?

- Genesis 6:11–13; 7:1–24

- Exodus 14:26–31

- Exodus 17:1–7

- 1 Peter 3:18–22

By all rights, Jonah should have perished in the storm-tossed sea, but to the contrary, in its very depths, his life was actually saved—and in the belly of a great fish no less. Even so, his sinking under the waves, going down into the water, was a direct result of his rebellion, and in that way, it symbolizes God's ultimate judgment, which is death, on *everyone* who rebels against God and doesn't repent. We can rightly take Jonah's sinking in the sea as a symbol of death because of the language used in the story itself. Three days and three nights, Jonah's duration in the sea, was the time frame used in the ancient world to confirm that someone was really dead, not merely unconscious or in a state of shock.

✦ The water holds great significance, but so does the direction it carries Jonah—down. That's where water takes anyone who can't swim or boat successfully. When we see the expression "go down," or "he went down" in Scripture, the words are often meant to communicate something significant. How does Psalm 88:3–7 reveal what this is?

"Hell is the end of every desire to flee from God."[13]

3. "JUST AS . . ." (1:17)

So by all rights, Jonah should no longer be alive. If the sea hadn't drowned him, certainly being swallowed by a fish would have done it. Yet, as we will see, both the sea and the creature that swallowed him are turned by God toward Jonah's salvation. But what's happening here has far greater significance than the rescue of a wayward prophet, a significance we learn about from the very words of the Lord Jesus himself:

> "Then some of the scribes and Pharisees answered him, saying, 'Teacher, we wish to see a sign from you.' But he answered them, 'An evil and adulterous generation seeks for a sign, but no sign will be given to it except the sign of the prophet Jonah. For just as Jonah was three days and three nights in the belly of the great fish, so will the Son of Man be three days and three nights in the heart of the earth.'" (Matthew 12:38–40)

✦ We're going to look more closely at the context of Jesus's words in Matthew 12 when we get to Week 10, but for now, let's focus on the implications of what he says here and how it ties back to Jonah. First, it is Jesus himself who says that what happened to Jonah was a sign. According to Jesus, what did Jonah's days beneath the sea signify? See also Acts 2:22–23.

✦ The fish represents hell and no doubt felt that way to the suffering Jonah. And perhaps his mind wandered unwillingly to thoughts of a fearsome sea creature called Leviathan. This creature, found in ancient myths, was a well-known symbol of evil, and for that reason, we might consider the great fish that swallowed Jonah another sign, this one pointing all the way to the end of time and what will happen then because of Jesus's death on the cross. What is this sign, according to Isaiah 27:1?

✦ Back up from the deep, onboard the ship, the mariners have been enjoying a radically different experience—the wonders of salvation. The storm has stopped, they are amazed by the power of God, and they express their awe-filled wonder in acts of worship. Jonah the guilty had been sacrificed, and through his sinking down, they'd been saved. According to Ephesians 2:11–16, how does what happened to the mariners also serve as a sign pointing to the work of Christ?

LET'S TALK

1. Talk about how the story of Jonah so far has enriched your understanding of man's sin, God's righteousness, and how Christ's death on the cross opened the way to salvation.

2. Jonah seems not to care what happens to the mariners. We too get so caught up in the drama of our lives that we often have little space in our hearts for the lost. It's hard to see ourselves clearly, but discouragement, despair, or frustration with God's ordering of our lives can serve as tipoffs that we are curved selfishly inward. How would you assess your heart right now? If change is needed, what will you do to redirect your focus upward and outward?

WEEK 5

DOWN IN THE DEPTHS

JONAH 2:1-6

We've seen how Jonah's descent into the sea is a picture of death, God's just punishment for unrepentant rebels. Now, this week and next, we'll linger with Jonah at the bottom of the sea as he recounts what happened to him inside the great fish. It's hard to imagine this odd setting because we've never experienced anything even close, but we can say with confidence that it was surely awful. No doubt Jonah couldn't see his hand in front of his face in the utter darkness, but he could feel and taste and smell. Perhaps he lapsed in and out of consciousness as the fish swam up and down the currents, swallowing gallons of fresh prey and sea water on top of Jonah. Sunday-school renderings often picture the fish's belly as a warm, dry cave-like setting, but the reality was more likely a hellish nightmare, with Jonah very near death inside that fish. Even so, he was sufficiently conscious to think and to pray, and his prayer is our primary focus this week.

1. THE MIGHTY SEA (2:1–6)

Jonah's attempts to run away from God haven't worked, as such attempts never do. Running from God leads only one direction—down. We've followed Jonah on his downward course all the way to rock bottom. Literally.

> "Then Jonah prayed to the Lord his God from the belly of the fish, saying,

'I called out to the Lord, out of my
distress,
and he answered me;
out of the belly of Sheol I cried,
and you heard my voice.
For you cast me into the deep,
into the heart of the seas,
and the flood surrounded me;
all your waves and your billows
passed over me.
Then I said, "I am driven away
from your sight;
yet I shall again look
upon your holy temple."
The waters closed in over me to take my life;
the deep surrounded me;
weeds were wrapped about my head
at the roots of the mountains.
I went down to the land
whose bars closed upon me forever;
yet you brought up my life from the pit,
O Lord my God.'" (vv. 1–6)

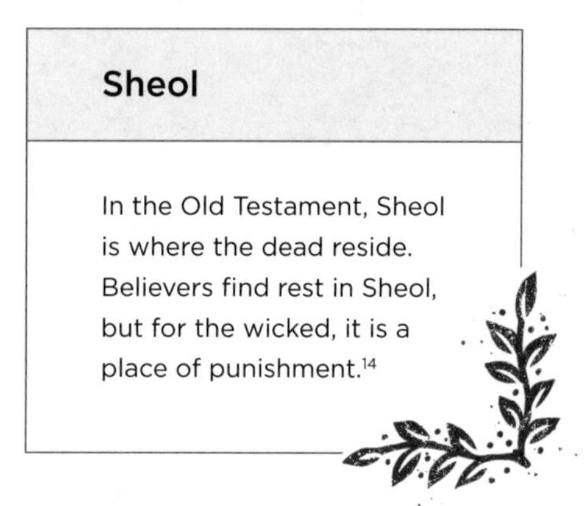

Sheol

In the Old Testament, Sheol is where the dead reside. Believers find rest in Sheol, but for the wicked, it is a place of punishment.[14]

Imprisoned at the bottom of the sea, Jonah is experiencing a foretaste of hell, of "Sheol" (v. 2), the place of the dead. In our day, we associate the sea with fun at the beach and boating adventures, but in ancient times, the sea was feared. While necessary for travel and commerce, it was associated with danger and chaos. Write down all the sea images you find in verses 1–6.

Revelation, the last book of the Bible, contains a lot of symbolism for the return of Christ at the end of the age and the new heavens and earth. What is symbolized by the sea imagery in Revelation 13:1–4 and 21:1–2?

2. CRY OF THE HEART (2:1–6)

Jonah does what lots of people do when death seems close—he prays. Yet his prayer is no attempt to bargain with God, something like, "If you get me out of this mess, I promise to be a good person." Nor is it a cry for release from the fish—not once in his prayer does Jonah ask for this.

It's clear that Jonah was well versed in the Psalms because he draws from several of them as he prays, including bits and pieces from each of the Psalms passages that follow (the specific portions Jonah draws from are italicized):

> "O Lord, how many are my foes!
> Many are rising against me;
> many are saying of my soul,
> 'There is no salvation for him in God.'
>
> But you, O Lord, are a shield about me,
> my glory, and the lifter of my head.
> *I cried aloud to the Lord,*
> *and he answered me* from his holy hill." (Psalm 3:1–4)
>
> "The cords of death encompassed me;
> the torrents of destruction assailed me;
> *the cords of Sheol entangled me*;
> the snares of death confronted me.
>
> *In my distress I called upon the Lord*;
> to my God I cried for help.
> From his temple he heard my voice,
> and my cry to him reached his ears." (Psalm 18:4–6)

"*I had said in my alarm,*
'I am cut off from your sight.'
But you heard the voice of my pleas for mercy
when I cried to you for help." (Psalm 31:22)

"Deep calls to deep
at the roar of your waterfalls;
all your breakers and your waves
have gone over me.
By day the LORD commands his steadfast love,
and at night his song is with me,
a prayer to the God of my life." (Psalm 42:7–8)

"Save me, O God!
For the waters have come up to my neck.
I sink in deep mire,
where there is no foothold;
I have come into deep waters,
and the flood sweeps over me.
I am weary with my crying out;
my throat is parched.
My eyes grow dim
with waiting for my God." (Psalm 69:1–3)

"*You have put me in the depths of the pit,*
in the regions dark and deep.
Your wrath lies heavy upon me,
and *you overwhelm me with all your waves.*" (Psalm 88:6–7)

How does Jonah's reference to these particular psalms provide insight into how his desperate situation is changing his heart and the way he views both himself and the Lord?

✦ Jonah well knows that the mariners had tossed him into the sea at his very own suggestion, but now, even though he nears the sleep of death, his heart and mind are waking up, and his entire perspective is changing. Whom does he now see as the cause of his plight?

✦ In last week's lesson we focused on how Jonah's going down into the sea points forward in time to the death of another prophet—the ultimate prophet—the Lord Jesus Christ. We know this from the words of Jesus himself, who said, "Just as Jonah was three days and three nights in the belly of the great fish, so will the Son of Man be three days and three nights in the heart of the earth" (Matthew 12:40). What does Jonah say in his prayer that further points to what Christ experienced in his suffering for sinners, as revealed in Matthew 27:46?

✦ Identify all the things that Jonah attributes directly to the Lord in verses 1–6.

3. GLIMMER OF HOPE (2:1–6)

Jonah's desperate cry is not without glimpses of hope. There is no need to assume these hints of hope were afterthoughts, tacked on long after his rescue as he recounts his experience. After all, hope is always the result of getting our eyes on God and praying.

- Identify Jonah's declarations of hope in verses 1–6.

- In Jonah's day, the Lord chose to set his presence in a man-made structure, first in the tabernacle and later in the grand temple built by King Solomon. The tabernacle and temple were where God's people brought sacrifices for sin and received cleansing and forgiveness. With this background in mind, what do you think Jonah is saying in verse 4 when he speaks of the temple?

- Jonah has no idea that he's going to be rescued from the fish at this point. In fact, death likely seems inevitable. So if physical survival isn't his hope, what is?

"Sometimes the very best thing that can happen to us is the very thing we most dread, for the simple reason that it strips away our self-reliance, humbles our pride, and removes from us every other hope save that of God. Sometimes this is what it takes for us to really pray."[15]

LET'S TALK

1. Jonah's dire circumstances prompted him to pray. At that point, prayer was all he *could* do. How does this change your perspective about the Lord and on the various troubles he brings into your life? How could this new perspective change the way you are praying about a current difficulty?

2. Jonah's newfound hope wasn't about getting out alive but about belonging to God eternally. Is your hope in the Lord rooted in him or more often in what you hope he will do in your day-to-day life? If your hope is more about the here and now, you don't have to hit rock bottom, like Jonah, to change. What available means of grace can you cultivate—such

as honesty with God, deep connections with fellow believers, and marinating in Scripture—to help reorient your hope?

WEEK 6

A REORIENTED HEART

JONAH 2:7-10

We are still with Jonah at the bottom of the sea as his life ebbs away. But even as Jonah's body draws near to death, his spiritual senses are coming back to life. His prayer reveals even more of a spiritual reawakening, which is what happens when someone rejects sin and self-centeredness and turns toward the Lord God. The biblical term for turning back to God is called "repentance." From Jonah we learn a good bit about repentance—how it happens and what comes as a result. A significant sin to repent of is idolatry. All through the Bible we find God's people falling into this sin, the worship of false gods. This week we're also going to cover the spiritual dangers of this particular sin, which tempts all of us at times, in one way or another.

1. REMEMBER! (2:7)

When our life is threatened, we instinctively fight to survive, frantically grasping at any and all prospects for deliverance. But if all our desperate attempts fail, we have no choice but to accept what's happening to us. Jonah has reached that point. His strength spent, his ability to withstand the contents of the fish's belly and breathe the fetid air fades away. But it's at this very point—accepting the approach of death—that his spiritual senses are quickened:

> "When my life was fainting away,
> I remembered the Lord." (v. 7a)

✦ Why do you think this particular moment led Jonah to remember the Lord?

Jonah's *remembering* marks the turning point in his heart. It's not that he'd forgotten God in an intellectual sense. It's that at some point, he'd lost his spiritual sensitivity, a discerning of God's presence and character that wells up in joy-filled worship and obedience. It's a reawakening of the fact that God is the be-all and end-all of everything.

✦ What insight do we get from Proverbs 3:34 to help us understand Jonah's remembering?

Jonah's remembering compelled him toward the Lord in prayer:

> "When my life was fainting away,
> I remembered the Lord,
> and my prayer came to you,
> into your holy temple." (v. 7)

✦ When Israel's grand temple in Jerusalem was completed and ready to be used for worship, King Solomon dedicated it to the Lord with a prayer. How do the words of Solomon's prayer in 1 Kings 8:27–30 help us understand Jonah's mention of the temple here in verse 7?

2. VAIN IDOLS (2:8)

Jonah's humbled condition and accompanying repentance give him spiritual clarity about sin:

> "Those who pay regard to vain idols
> forsake their hope of steadfast love." (v. 8)

The specific sin Jonah mentions here is idolatry, or idol worship. In ancient times, idols were statues in the shape of animals and objects that were believed to promote fertility and plentiful harvests. Idols in our day are much less visible but no less real. Today's idols are things like youth and beauty and materialism. Idols vary across time, but in every age, an idol is anything or anyone people trust or depend on in such a way as to push aside trust and dependence on the Lord.

Some Bible scholars think that Jonah's thoughts here in verse 8 were back on the mariners who'd tossed him into the sea. If you recall, each of those mariners had looked for rescue in his preferred god, or idol (take a look back at 1:5). But more likely, Jonah has God's own people, Israel, in mind here. As his heart returns to the Lord, his thoughts would quite naturally turn toward the Lord's people as well. And we see throughout the Old Testament that idolatry was Israel's besetting sin, generation after generation.

"Hast Thou Heard Him, Seen Him, Known Him?"

Hast thou heard Him, seen Him, known Him?
Is not thine a captured heart?
Chief among ten thousand own Him;
Joyful choose the better part.

Captivated by His beauty,
Worthy tribute haste to bring;
Let His peerless worth constrain thee,
Crown Him now unrivaled King. . . .

What has stripped the seeming beauty
From the idols of the earth?
Not a sense of right or duty,
But the sight of peerless worth.

Not the crushing of those idols,
With its bitter void and smart;
But the beaming of His beauty,
The unveiling of His heart. . . .

Draw and win and fill completely,
Till the cup o'erflow the brim;
What have we to do with idols
Who have companied with Him?[16]

Too, we know that Jonah was a prophet in Israel, and prophets had the responsibility to call God's people to repent of their sin. So Jonah's words here in verse 8 are another indicator of his restoration, a return to his God-given calling.

- Jonah declares that idol worshipers "forsake their hope of steadfast love" (v. 8). The Hebrew word translated here as "steadfast love" is *hesed*. It's an important word in the Old Testament because it's used primarily to describe the Lord's love, kindness, and good intentions toward his people. It is also translated as "mercy" or "faithful love." With this in mind, what do you think Jonah means by his declaration in verse 8?

- What do Isaiah 44:12–20 and Jeremiah 2:11–13 add to your understanding of Jonah's declaration in verse 8?

"If 'idolatry' is the characteristic and summary Old Testament word for our drift from God, then 'desires' . . . is the characteristic and summary New Testament word for the same drift. Both are shorthand for the problem of human beings."[17]

Those who "pay regard" to idols miss true blessing, Jonah says. What do you think it means to pay regard to an idol? Identify some examples either from Scripture or from personal observation and experience.

3. TOTAL TURNAROUND (2:9–10)

Jonah rejects all false gods because nothing can compare to the God his heart now remembers.

> "But I with the voice of thanksgiving
> will sacrifice to you;
> what I have vowed I will pay.
> Salvation belongs to the LORD!" (v. 9)

Despite the fact that Jonah is still inside the fish, still near death, he pours out thanks to God and makes a powerful declaration about him. Given the circumstances and timing, what does this indicate about the nature of genuine repentance?

When Jonah speaks in verse 9 of what he will do in the future—make sacrifices—this most likely isn't because he believes God will rescue him alive from the fish. Rather, he is merely acknowledging his guilt and his need for spiritual cleansing—another mark of genuine repentance. The sacrifices he vows to offer (v. 9) are tied to how God's people experienced cleansing and forgiveness under the old covenant, the time before

Christ atoned for sins on the cross. Guilty sinners brought animals to the temple as a sacrificial offering for their sin, because "under the law [the old covenant] almost everything is purified with blood, and without the shedding of blood there is no forgiveness of sins" (Hebrews 9:22). The blood of those animals substituted as payment until Christ offered himself once for all time to pay for sins. (Christ's atoning work applies not just to those who live after his sacrifice, but to all who lived before then as well.)

✦ How do Jonah's words in verse 9 tie back to the mariners in 1:16?

✦ Given his circumstances, what does Jonah mean when he declares that "salvation belongs to the Lord" (v. 9)?

Suddenly Jonah is spun around and projected upward. If he was conscious at this point, he certainly had no idea what was happening:

> "And the Lord spoke to the fish, and it vomited Jonah out upon the dry land." (v. 10)

The God who'd cast Jonah beneath the sea and into the mouth of a fish, taking the prophet to the brink of death, then guided that very same fish to save Jonah's life.

✦ The Lord didn't rescue Jonah because he repented. In other words, Jonah didn't "earn" divine rescue. Scripture overall makes clear that God doesn't work that way.

We don't earn his blessings, nor can we negotiate for his favor. How then can we best understand God's work in Jonah's life through this chain of events?

LET'S TALK

1. What in your life are you tempted to idolize? We can make an idol of our family, our job, our health or appearance, our money, and even our spiritual giftedness. Discuss ways to recognize when something good has crossed over into idolatry. Include in your discussion ways to keep otherwise good things from turning into idols.

2. Talk about a time when God let you suffer consequences for sin. How did it change your heart toward the Lord, and how did the suffering change you?

WEEK 7

PREACH IT, JONAH!

JONAH 3:1–5a

Jonah, back on dry ground, is alive but no doubt physically weak. Very likely his thirty-six hours inside the fish has altered his appearance (as we'd expect of anyone who'd spent three days inside the digestive system of a living creature). More importantly, it has altered his heart. The Jonah we're going to see this week is a changed man. Gone is his determination to live life on his own terms, to run away from God and his word. Jonah has always been a *prophet of God*, but now he is *God's prophet*. We've already seen how the Lord prepared Jonah to carry his message; now we're going to see that he's prepared the Ninevites to receive it. Yet our primary focus isn't so much the changes to Jonah or the changes coming to the Ninevites as what those changes say about God himself—his power and grace and mercy. All that is put on display for us this week.

1. THE GOD OF SECOND CHANCES (3:1–2)

The Lord's grace is relentless. That's one of the most vital takeaways from the book of Jonah, and we see it here as he calls the prophet a second time:

> "Then the word of the Lord came to Jonah the second time, saying, 'Arise, go to Nineveh, that great city, and call out against it the message that I tell you.'" (vv. 1–2)

A *second time*—some of us know firsthand the joy contained in that phrase. When we've made a mess of our lives through sin or unwise choices, we're tempted to think we're stuck with Plan B. If only we'd obeyed . . . If only we'd done this and not that . . . *If only*. We learn from Jonah that under God, there is no Plan B. We are exactly where we are today—even if it seems like the belly of a fish—because the Lord is directing our steps to accomplish all he has planned for our lives. God had plans for Jonah, and God worked in and through the prophet and his circumstances to bring them to pass.

How do the following passages deepen your understanding of how the Lord works in and through our own choices for his purposes?

- Job 42:1–2

- Proverbs 16:9

- Acts 17:24–28

- Romans 8:28–30

What subtle difference do you note between God's first call of Jonah (1:2) and the second call here in 3:2?

This is a good time to remind ourselves why the Lord calls Nineveh a "great city" (v. 2). First, it was great in size. This military capital of the Assyrian Empire was a very large city with a population of 120,000 (see 4:11). Second, it was great in power. The Assyrians were world-renowned for military aggression and ruthless treatment of their enemies, and while its military tactics had been somewhat subdued in Jonah's day, they were still widely feared by surrounding nations. Third, Nineveh was great because it was important to God, which is clear from the fact that he sends Jonah there to preach in his name.

"The Lord comes a second time to all who are his true children."[18]

2. FAITHFUL PREACHING (3:3–4)

The Lord has given Jonah specific instructions. He is to journey to Nineveh and convey in no uncertain terms God's message.

> "So Jonah arose and went to Nineveh, according to the word of the LORD. Now Nineveh was an exceedingly great city, three days' journey in breadth. Jonah began to go into the city, going a day's journey. And he called out, 'Yet forty days, and Nineveh shall be overthrown!'" (vv. 3–4)

We notice immediately how Jonah responds differently to God's call this time. No quibbling, no quarreling. The Lord said, "Arise, go," so Jonah "arose and went."

✦ How would you describe the differences in Jonah's heart that would compel him to press through his physical weakness and his understandable qualms about going in among the fierce Ninevites with the Lord's message—a message that could be perceived as hostile?

✦ Jonah spends a day getting the lay of the land, and as he gets into the heart of the city, he calls out the message the Lord has given him, "Yet forty days, and Nineveh shall be overthrown" (v. 4), a message of just eight words. How would you characterize the tone of this message?

God's Wrath

"The preaching of divine wrath serves as a black velvet backdrop that causes the diamond of God's mercy to shine brighter than ten thousand suns. It is upon the dark canvas of divine wrath that the splendor of His saving grace most fully radiates. Preaching the wrath of God most brilliantly showcases His gracious mercy toward sinners. . . . Every preacher must declare the wrath of God or marginalize His holiness, love, and righteousness. Because God is holy, He is separated from all sin and utterly opposed to every sinner. Because God is love, He delights in purity and must, of necessity, hate all that is unholy. Because God is righteous, He must punish the sin that violates His holiness."[19]

Forty is a significant number in the Bible. It is "often used in Scripture for times of preparation or warning" and it "speaks of a definitive time established by God before his coming either in judgment or in grace."[20]

- The message Jonah delivers is given not as an appeal but as a warning. How does the content of Jonah's short message differ from so many of the messages and sermons preached about the Lord in our churches today?

- Many years later, another prophet, Nahum, called out against Nineveh after the city had once again declined, fallen away from the Lord, and finally reached the peak of its terrifying power and depravity. Read Nahum 3:1–7. How does this later prophecy reveal what God's current message through Jonah is designed to spare them?

- How does Romans 2:6–11 help us understand why Jonah warning the Ninevites of God's wrath was not harshness but rather a demonstration of God's kindness?

3. A SURPRISING RESPONSE (3:5a)

It's likely that no one was more surprised than Jonah with how the Ninevites responded to his message:

> "And the people of Nineveh believed God." (v. 5a)

✦ Although Jonah has delivered the message, whom do the Ninevites actually hear?

✦ No pretty words, no prosperity promises, yet the people believed what Jonah told them. We'd think they'd need more information as to the *whats* and the *hows* and the *whys*, but Jonah stuck to the eight words God had instructed him to preach. How do the following passages show us why such a change was possible?

- Isaiah 65:1–2

- Romans 10:14–17

- Galatians 3:5

The Ninevites are getting their first real look at the one true God, and what they glimpse is not only his pending wrath but, amazingly, his mercy. They are waking up to the fact that God is under no obligation to warn them. He has every right to pass judgment on them with no warning whatsoever, like he did back in Genesis 19 when he judged Sodom and Gomorrah with sudden destruction. The Ninevites have begun to ask themselves, "Do you presume on the riches of his kindness and forbearance and patience, not knowing that God's kindness is meant to lead you to repentance?" (Romans 2:4).

LET'S TALK

1. There is no Plan B with God. How does this truth reshape your view of your past missteps and sins?

2. What about Jonah's message to the Ninevites and the way they responded encourages you to share the gospel with unbelievers in your life? How and to whom will you share with new boldness?

WEEK 8

SACKCLOTH AND ASHES

JONAH 3:5-10

Jonah had traveled a good distance into the city of Nineveh before preaching God's word, far enough in that his message would be picked up and spread from street to street, outward to the farthest edges of the city walls. From what we've seen, his strategy worked. The Ninevites believed Jonah when he said that the city would be overthrown in just forty days. And they recognized that wrapped up in Jonah's warning was God's mercy. How do we know? We can be confident in that assessment because of what comes next in our story. The way the Ninevites respond, both in the words they say and the actions they take, reveals that the Spirit worked through God's word to open their hearts to see truth. That's how salvation happens in every age—through the word and the Spirit. And genuine salvation goes hand in hand with repentance. We can't help but notice by now that repentance is a key theme in the book of Jonah. The pagan mariners were first in the story to turn from sin to God. Afterward we witnessed the repentance of Jonah himself, which came about when he recognized his desperate need of God to save him. Now we're going to see a widescale repentance as the entire city of Nineveh discovers the one true God.

1. TRUE FAITH (3:5–8)

The Ninevites have heard Jonah. They have forty days—not much more than a month—until life as they've known and enjoyed it will cease. And their response is swift:

> "The people of Nineveh believed God. They called for a fast and put on sack-cloth, from the greatest of them to the least of them. The word reached the king

> of Nineveh, and he arose from his throne, removed his robe, covered himself with sackcloth, and sat in ashes. And he issued a proclamation and published through Nineveh, 'By the decree of the king and his nobles: Let neither man nor beast, herd nor flock, taste anything. Let them not feed or drink water, but let man and beast be covered with sackcloth, and let them call out mightily to God. Let everyone turn from his evil way and from the violence that is in his hands.'" (vv. 5–8)

The ordering of these events seems backward, the people calling for a fast and then, afterward, the king following along. But most likely the king first issued his edict, and then the citizens of Nineveh carried it out. The storyteller has reversed the order purposefully. "By putting the people's response ahead of the king's proclamation, the author underscores the immediacy of the people's response and that they are responding to Jonah's message, not just to the king's command."[21]

✦ Look at the king's edict in verse 8, which includes even the animals. In addition to fasting, what components of genuine repentance do you see in his edict? If you aren't sure what those components are, take a look at Psalm 51, a prayer of repentance.

✦ People often fasted during times of personal or national mourning and sorrow for sin. Those who were fasting wore clothing made from a coarse fabric typically used for grain sacks, and during the fast they would sit outside in a pile of ashes. Led by the king, the Ninevites did all these things. What do these actions reveal about their heart response to Jonah's message?

- In the Bible we find other national fasts initiated by leaders, such as the one led by Ezra the priest. According to Ezra 8:21, what is fasting intended to accomplish in one's heart?

What we see here in Nineveh is an amazing display of repentance in which all the people, from the king on down, turn away from sin and look wholeheartedly toward God. And the people get specific, not merely acknowledging sin in general but the specific sin they were known for—violence.

> *"It is through repentance that many of God's choicest graces enter our experience. If each of us took stock of our habitual sins and earnestly pleaded with God in persistent prayer, relying on the power of his grace, then the freedom we would gain from breaking just one sinful habit would revolutionize our lives."*[22]

2. JONAH AS SIGN (3:9)

We see something else in the king's words that accompanies true repentance—hope.

> "Who knows? God may turn and relent and turn from his fierce anger, so that we may not perish." (v. 9)

- Which attribute of God does the king acknowledge here, and which attribute does he hope to experience?

The Ninevites' eyes have been opened to see the Lord for who he is—holy, righteous, and all-powerful—and as a result, they see the true nature of their sin—unrighteous and deserving of death. And the fact that Lord had overcome a reluctant prophet to do it gives them hope. From the words of Jesus himself, it seems that that the people of the city knew about Jonah's underwater experience and the miracle of his deliverance:

> "Some of the scribes and Pharisees answered him, saying, 'Teacher, we wish to see a sign from you.' But he answered them, 'An evil and adulterous generation seeks for a sign, but no sign will be given to it except the sign of the prophet Jonah. For just as Jonah was three days and three nights in the belly of the great fish, so will the Son of Man be three days and three nights in the heart of the earth. The men of Nineveh will rise up at the judgment with this generation and condemn it, for they repented at the preaching of Jonah, and behold, something greater than Jonah is here.'" (Matthew 12:38–41)

What's going on there in Matthew is that some Pharisees, religious leaders in Jesus's day, had demanded that Jesus prove his identity with a miraculous sign because they refused to see that Jesus himself was all the sign they needed. But because those Pharisees had no faith, they wouldn't have believed him no matter what he did. The Ninevites, on the other hand, with nothing more than the fish-scarred Jonah and his eight-word message, believed.

How would knowing of Jonah's underwater experience have served as a sign of hope for the Ninevites?

The way in which the Ninevites responded to Jonah was also a sign, one for the people of Israel in Jonah's day who were so easily entrenched in idol worship and refused to repent and turn back to God. The fact that the Ninevites heard God's word and turned to him in true repentance and faith should have shamed Israel to repent of their own sins.

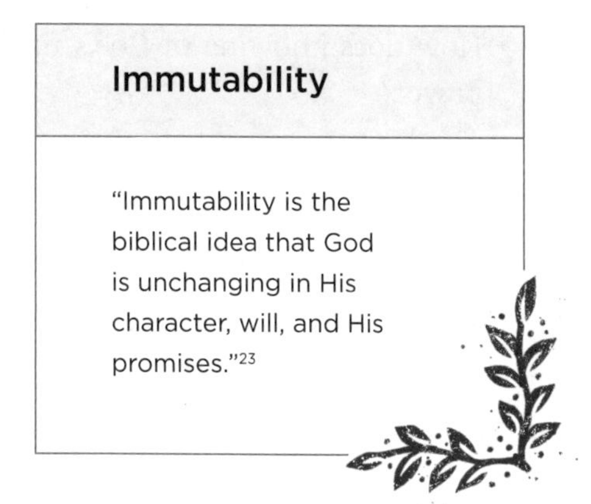

3. GOD RELENTS (3:10)

God blesses the repentant Ninevites, and what they've been hoping for comes true:

> "When God saw what they did, how they turned from their evil way, God relented of the disaster that he had said he would do to them, and he did not do it." (v. 10)

In order to interpret verse 10 rightly, it's important that we understand how the Bible uses language to show us who God is. The Bible writers frequently use *anthropomorphisms* to describe the Lord's ways and works. An anthropomorphism is a literary device that applies characteristics of human beings to something that isn't actually human. So when the storyteller says that "God saw," he is using anthropomorphic language because God doesn't actually have eyes. The same type of language is used where we read that "God relented." We know from elsewhere in the Bible that God doesn't relent—he doesn't change his mind. In other words, the actions of human beings do not determine what God does or doesn't do.

✦ To get a deeper grasp of God's unchangeableness—what theologians define as his *immutability*—read Numbers 23:19, 1 Samuel 15:29, and James 1:17. Why is this truth about God comforting for Christians?

✦ How does knowing of God's unchangeableness shape or reshape our approach to prayer?

Bible study principle: Scripture interprets Scripture.

So how do we explain what actually happens here in verse 10? The pending destruction of Nineveh was not an empty threat. If the Ninevites had not relented, they would have experienced God's judgment in forty days' time. Instead, they were changed in order to experience God's mercy. In other words, God doesn't change his mind—he changes people. Here's how one Jonah scholar explains it:

> It was wicked, violent, unrighteous, atheistical, proud, and luxurious Nineveh which God threatened to destroy. A city sitting in sack-cloth and ashes, humbled . . . —a Nineveh like that—God had never threatened. *That* Nineveh he visited not with ruin. He had never said he would.[24]

God never changes. His wrath is sure and fixed. His mercy is sure and fixed. The question is which one we will align ourselves under.

✦ What does the Lord's response to the Ninevites' repentance reveal about his character?

LET'S TALK

1. The Ninevites repented after hearing Jonah's brief eight-word message. To what do you attribute this incredible response? In our efforts to be winsome, it's tempting when we share the gospel with unbelievers to go heavy on God's love and go light on sin and the need for repentance. How does what happened in Nineveh reshape our approach to evangelism?

2. What do we learn about the nature of true repentance from the Ninevites? See if you can identify an area in your life where a wholehearted repentance is needed. If something comes to mind, what will your repentance look like?

WEEK 9

GRACE FOR BACKSLIDERS

JONAH 4:1–4

Growing our faith is typically a lifelong process, a road we walk with some regrettable stops or detours along the way. That was certainly true of Jonah. We've watched as he rebelled against God but then repented of his rebellion and took concrete steps forward in faith and obedience. Now, when we get to the last chapter of the story, he takes a step—a big step—backward. But through all Jonah's inconsistency, one thing is consistent from beginning to end, and that's God's grace. Not once in the whole story does the Lord fail to show Jonah kindness and mercy. As we see what unfolds this week, we can't help but look with astonishment at Jonah's behavior, when he acts more like a petulant child than a privileged prophet. But the truth is, we're actually a good bit like Jonah sometimes (maybe a lot of the time). And we're meant to know that the grace and mercy God gives Jonah, God gives to us too.

1. JONAH THROWS A TANTRUM (4:1–2)

The Jonah at the beginning of chapter 4 seems very different from the Jonah we saw just two short chapters ago, the Jonah who'd offered praise and thanksgiving for God's salvation. How human he is! Surely we can see our own spiritual ups and downs reflected in Jonah's changeable moods.

> "But it displeased Jonah exceedingly, and he was angry. And he prayed to the Lord and said, 'O Lord, is not this what I said when I was yet in my country? That is why I made haste to flee to Tarshish; for I knew that you are a gracious

> God and merciful, slow to anger and abounding in steadfast love, and relenting from disaster.'" (vv. 1–2)

✦ We're not left to interpret how Jonah is feeling—he's just plain angry. Verse 1 points us to the reason. What has so displeased him?

Jonah is saying to God, "What you've done is exactly why I didn't want to come here, why I ran away from you. Yet here I am."

> *"We need to learn that we are not sufficient to pass on the appropriateness of the outcome, nor are we responsible for it. We are responsible only for performing the whole will of God."*[25]

In his complaint, Jonah draws his description of the Lord from Exodus 34:6–7. That's where God revealed himself to Moses on Mount Sinai as Israel's covenant Lord:

> "The Lord . . . proclaimed, 'The Lord, the Lord, a God merciful and gracious, slow to anger, and abounding in steadfast love and faithfulness, keeping steadfast love for thousands, forgiving iniquity and transgression and sin, but who will by no means clear the guilty, visiting the iniquity of the fathers on the children and the children's children, to the third and the fourth generation.'" (Exodus 34:6–7)

✦ Note the times and ways God has been true to his character—merciful, gracious, and slow to anger—so far in the story to:

- Jonah:

- the Ninevites:

Another angry man is found in a parable Jesus told about a father who had two sons. Read Luke 15:11–32. What connection can you make between the anger of the older son in Jesus's parable and Jonah's anger here?

As you consider how Jonah prays here in verses 1–2, what would you say is the root of his anger?

2. WHEN BITTERNESS BOILS OVER (4:3)

Through Jonah's whining complaint of a prayer, he has worked himself into a fit:

> "Therefore now, O Lord, please take my life from me, for it is better for me to die than to live." (v. 3)

✦ Perhaps Jonah really did wish to die, but just as easily his words might be a pitiful expression of bitterness. Asaph was another Old Testament figure who experienced bitterness for similar reasons. In his case, bitterness came not because God saved undeserving sinners but because sinners seem to profit from sin at the expense of God's own people. Read Psalm 73. What changes Asaph's outlook, and how does it change?

✦ Summarize how the Lord has "failed" to meet Jonah's expectations.

3. GRACE UPON GRACE (4:4)

God has every right to do exactly what Jonah demands—take his life away, right then and there. But the God who is gracious and merciful, abounding in steadfast love, and (unlike Jonah) slow to anger responds with a question instead:

> "And the LORD said, 'Do you do well to be angry?'" (v. 4)

Sprinkled throughout the Bible are occurrences of the Lord asking people questions. We see it with another discouraged prophet on the run, Elijah, when the Lord found him and asked, "What are you doing here, Elijah?" (1 Kings 19:9). Such divine questioning wasn't reserved only for God's people, as we see when the Lord met the runaway Egyptian slave Hagar in the wilderness: "Hagar, servant of Sarai, where have you come from and where are you going?" (Genesis 16:8). And in the New Testament Jesus frequently posed questions to his followers, as the Gospels attest.

✦ As you consider the Lord's question of Jonah as well as these other examples, what seems to be God's purpose in this approach?

✦ Jonah never answers the Lord's question, at least not that we're given to see. But much later in history, the apostle Paul offers an answer to those who take issue with God's ways. Read Romans 9:14–24. Based on what Paul says there, how should Jonah have answered the Lord's question, "Do you do well to be angry?" (v. 4).

Jonah said he was angry enough to die. We'd never have that thought, we think, but the truth is, we do. When the Lord doesn't meet our expectations, fulfill our dreams, or work out our problems in our time frames, we can find ourselves tempted to escape our pain and frustration—to escape him—by indulging in some form of sin. And what is sin, but a move toward death?

LET'S TALK

1. A well-meaning friend might say something like, "It's okay to be angry at God—he can take it." Discuss why this is unbiblical counsel. How does this week's lesson make that clear?

2. Are there things in the Bible about God and his ways that you struggle to understand or accept? Discuss why the approach given in Proverbs 30:5, James 4:6–8, and 1 Peter 5:6–8 is vital for finding answers to your own perplexities about God's ways and peace in your struggle.

WEEK 10

A PLANT, A WORM, AND A HOT EAST WIND

JONAH 4:5–11

We left Jonah in a very bad mood, and as we're about to see, he's still in that same frame of mind—angry and bitter. Ironically, success is what underlies his bad mood. For most of us, such moods are brought on by failure. After running away from God's call to preach in Nineveh, Jonah repented, came to the city, and delivered the message God had given him. Wonder of wonders, the Ninevites heard with their hearts and turned to the Lord in faith! Yet that's exactly why Jonah is angry. He did what the Lord had called him to do, but in his heart of hearts, it's clear that he hoped these longtime enemies of Israel would reject God's grace and experience judgment instead. We learn from God's dealings with Jonah that God uses both the failures and the successes of our own lives to expose what's really going on in our hearts. And as we come to the end of the story, we can't help but be awed by all we've learned about God's mercy, compassion, and relentless grace.

1. COMFORT AT LAST (4:5–6)

No doubt the newly converted Ninevites have lots of questions about this great God they are just getting to know, but the only one available to teach them bails:

> "Jonah went out of the city and sat to the east of the city and made a booth for himself there. He sat under it in the shade, till he should see what would become of the city." (v. 5)

Ancient Nineveh was situated in modern-day Iraq, in the district of Mosul. The summer climate is hot and arid, with temperatures climbing above 100 degrees Fahrenheit.

That Jonah would leave the comforts available inside the city to sit outside in the heat shows just how resentful he was.

✦ What do you think he is hoping to see as he sits there in his booth?

"Jonah was a discredit to the name of the God of grace he professed to serve. God had now sent his last messenger of providence. The word of the Lord had not come to Jonah a third time. Now, Jonah must decide: Disobedience or Commitment? We simply do not know which time God speaks to us will be the last time. We do well to assume this time is the last time—and commit ourselves to the Lord while he still speaks."[26]

Booths were temporary shelters, and Jonah likely constructed his booth from whatever ground materials he could find—palm fronds and various plants. As we can imagine, the shade it provided would not have been much help against the searing heat. Once again, the Lord provides:

> "Now the Lord God appointed a plant and made it come up over Jonah, that it might be a shade over his head, to save him from his discomfort. So Jonah was exceedingly glad because of the plant." (v. 6)

The plant was likely the castor oil plant, which has very large leaves. The plant grows very quickly and stands upright on a stalk.

What is indicated about Jonah's heart from the fact that this is the first (and only) time in the story that he is glad?

2. EASY COME, EASY GO (4:7–8)

Jonah's gladness is short-lived. After a pleasant night, the new day brings an end to his comfort:

> "But when dawn came up the next day, God appointed a worm that attacked the plant, so that it withered. When the sun rose, God appointed a scorching east wind, and the sun beat down on the head of Jonah so that he was faint. And he asked that he might die and said, 'It is better for me to die than to live.'" (vv. 7–8)

The worm was likely a type of moth. The dry, hot wind from the east, which meteorologists call "sirocco," still occurs in that region today, and it causes all living creatures to languish.

Sirocco

"During the period of a sirocco the temperature rises steeply. . . . At times every scrap of moisture seems to have been extracted from the air, so that one has the curious feeling that one's skin has been drawn much tighter than usual. Sirocco days are peculiarly trying to the temper and tend to make even the mildest people irritable and fretful and to snap at one another for apparently no reason at all."[27] The apostle James, in his New Testament letter, likens the effects of these dreaded winds to what happens to worldly, wealthy people: "The sun rises with its scorching heat and withers the grass; its flower falls, and its beauty perishes. So also will the rich man fade away in the midst of his pursuits" (James 1:11).

The Lord's activity is the focal point of these two verses, just like in chapter 1, where the Lord "hurled" the wind upon the sea (1:4). Here, as well as earlier in the story, we're told that the Lord *appoints*. From the verses that follow, jot down the Lord's *appointing* work throughout the story of Jonah.

- 1:17

- 4:6

- 4:7

- 4:8

- What do you think these appointments were designed to accomplish?

✦ What does this section teach us about God's purposes in sometimes taking away the very blessings he gives?

3. THE GOD WHO PITIES (4:9–11)

The prophet sits helplessly in the unbearable heat. The Lord's appointments have drawn out Jonah's anger afresh, preparing his heart to hear the word of the Lord once again:

> "But God said to Jonah, 'Do you do well to be angry for the plant?' And he said, 'Yes, I do well to be angry, angry enough to die.' And the LORD said, 'You pity the plant, for which you did not labor, nor did you make it grow, which came into being in a night and perished in a night. And should not I pity Nineveh, that great city, in which there are more than 120,000 persons who do not know their right hand from their left, and also much cattle?'" (vv. 9–11)

> *"God's questions are meant to teach us something, or to expose to us our inner selves when we are guilty of sin or disobedience. . . . So whenever we read the Bible and come across God asking a question, we ought to ask ourselves, 'Is God addressing that question to me, and if so what am I meant to learn from it?'"*[28]

✦ The Ninevites were Israel's enemies, as we know, and surely their salvation has contributed to Jonah's resentment, especially that God has sent him to have a part in it. But the plant and the worm and the wind reveal another reason for Jonah's anger. How has the Lord exposed through these means what Jonah really cares about, and thus why Jonah is unable to share the Lord's pity for the Ninevites?

✦ The Ninevites "do not know their right hand from their left"; in other words, they've had no knowledge about God until now, and what they know now is just a beginning. How does the Lord's self-description, which Jonah recited in verse 2, enable us to understand what is meant by the Lord's "pity"?

✦ How does the ending of the story—the mention of the cattle in Nineveh—underscore the attributes of God revealed in this chapter?

Jesus is why the story of Jonah matters.

The end of the story leaves us wanting more, doesn't it? Did Jonah respond to the Lord? We want to hear him declare, as he did in chapter 2, "Salvation belongs to the Lord!" (2:9). But we don't. We have no idea what ultimately happened to this intriguing prophet. Even so, he left a tremendously significant mark on the world through the words of Jesus. Jesus is why the story of Jonah matters:

> "An evil and adulterous generation seeks for a sign, but no sign will be given to it except the sign of the prophet Jonah. For just as Jonah was three days and three nights in the belly of the great fish, so will the Son of Man be three days and three nights in the heart of the earth. The men of Nineveh will rise up at the judgment with this generation and condemn it, for they repented at the preaching of Jonah, and behold, something greater than Jonah is here." (Matthew 12:39–41)

Jonah the prophet ran away from God's call to preach. Jesus the divine prophet ran toward it, and not only that—he fulfilled the message that was preached. Jonah's "death" in the sea was a sign of Jesus's death on the cross. Jonah's rescue from the fish was a sign of Jesus's resurrection. And the salvation of Nineveh through Jonah's preaching was a sign of the salvation made possible for every one of God's enemies through Christ. "Repent," Jesus says, "for the kingdom of heaven is at hand" (Matthew 4:17).

LET'S TALK

1. God sent a plant to comfort Jonah, and then he sent a worm and a wind to take away that comfort. Describe a time in your life when you experienced something similar—a God-given gift subsequently taken away by the very God who gave it. How did you respond, and what did you learn about the Lord and your own heart?

2. Discuss how the story of Jonah exposes our tendency toward self-centeredness. If we find ourselves regularly frustrated with life, could this be the root? If you could write an ending for Jonah as his response to the last scene in the story, what would you have him do by way of repentance?

3. As we come to the end of Jonah, note what you've learned or what's affected you most about

- the character of God:

- the gospel of salvation through Jesus Christ:

- the path of discipleship:

Chronology of Old Testament Kings and Prophets[29]

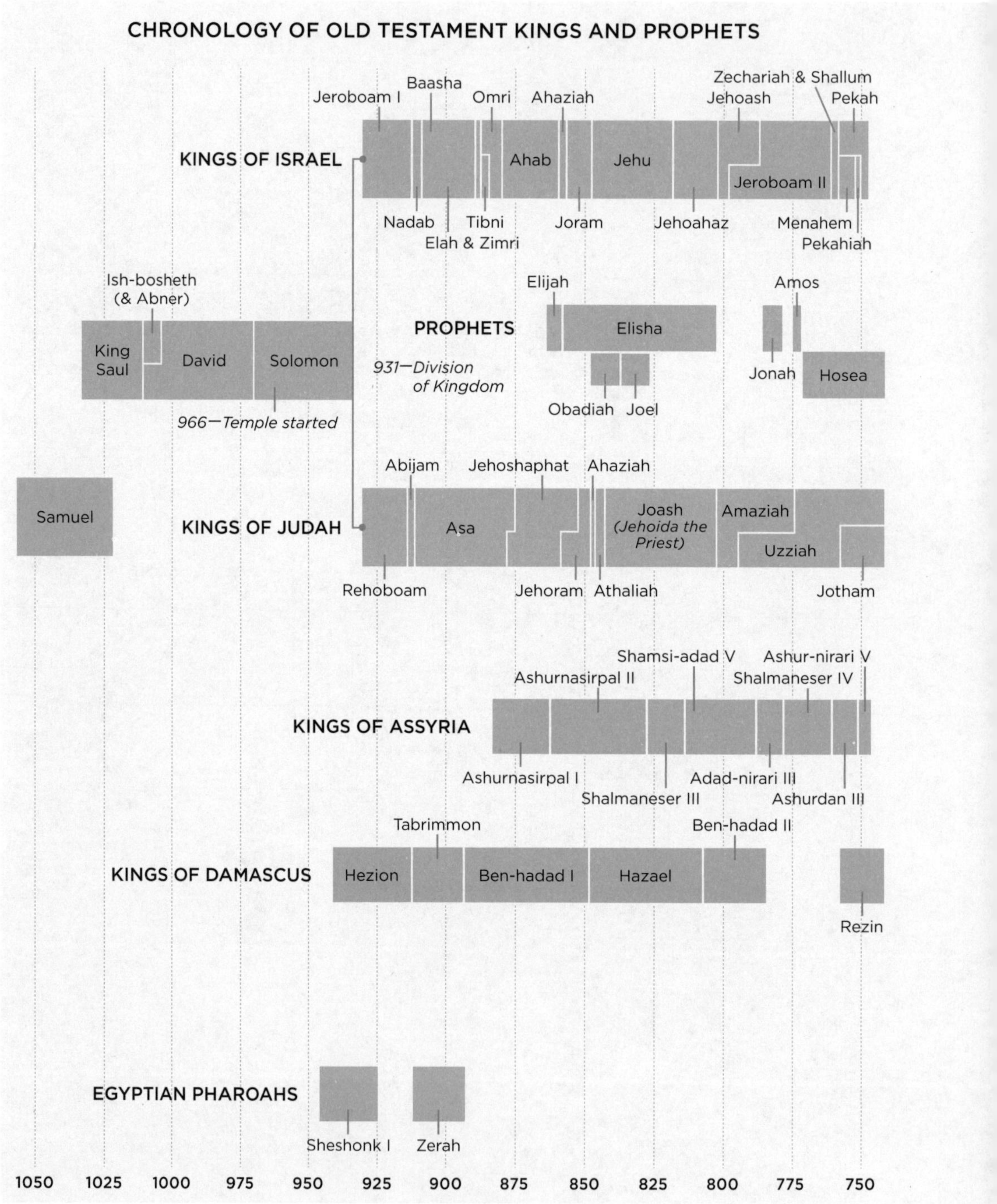

CHRONOLOGY OF OLD TESTAMENT KINGS AND PROPHETS

KINGS OF ISRAEL

Jeroboam I
Baasha
Omri
Ahaziah
Zechariah & Shallum
Jehoash
Pekah
Ahab
Jehu
Jeroboam II
Nadab
Tibni
Elah & Zimri
Joram
Jehoahaz
Menahem
Pekahiah

PROPHETS

Elijah
Elisha
Obadiah
Joel
Amos
Jonah
Hosea

Ish-bosheth (& Abner)
King Saul
David
Solomon
966—Temple started
931—Division of Kingdom

Samuel

KINGS OF JUDAH

Abijam
Jehoshaphat
Ahaziah
Asa
Joash *(Jehoida the Priest)*
Amaziah
Uzziah
Rehoboam
Jehoram
Athaliah
Jotham

KINGS OF ASSYRIA

Shamsi-adad V
Ashur-nirari V
Ashurnasirpal II
Shalmaneser IV
Ashurnasirpal I
Adad-nirari III
Shalmaneser III
Ashurdan III

KINGS OF DAMASCUS

Tabrimmon
Ben-hadad II
Hezion
Ben-hadad I
Hazael
Rezin

EGYPTIAN PHAROAHS

Sheshonk I
Zerah

1050 1025 1000 975 950 925 900 875 850 825 800 775 750

CHRONOLOGY OF OLD TESTAMENT KINGS AND PROPHETS

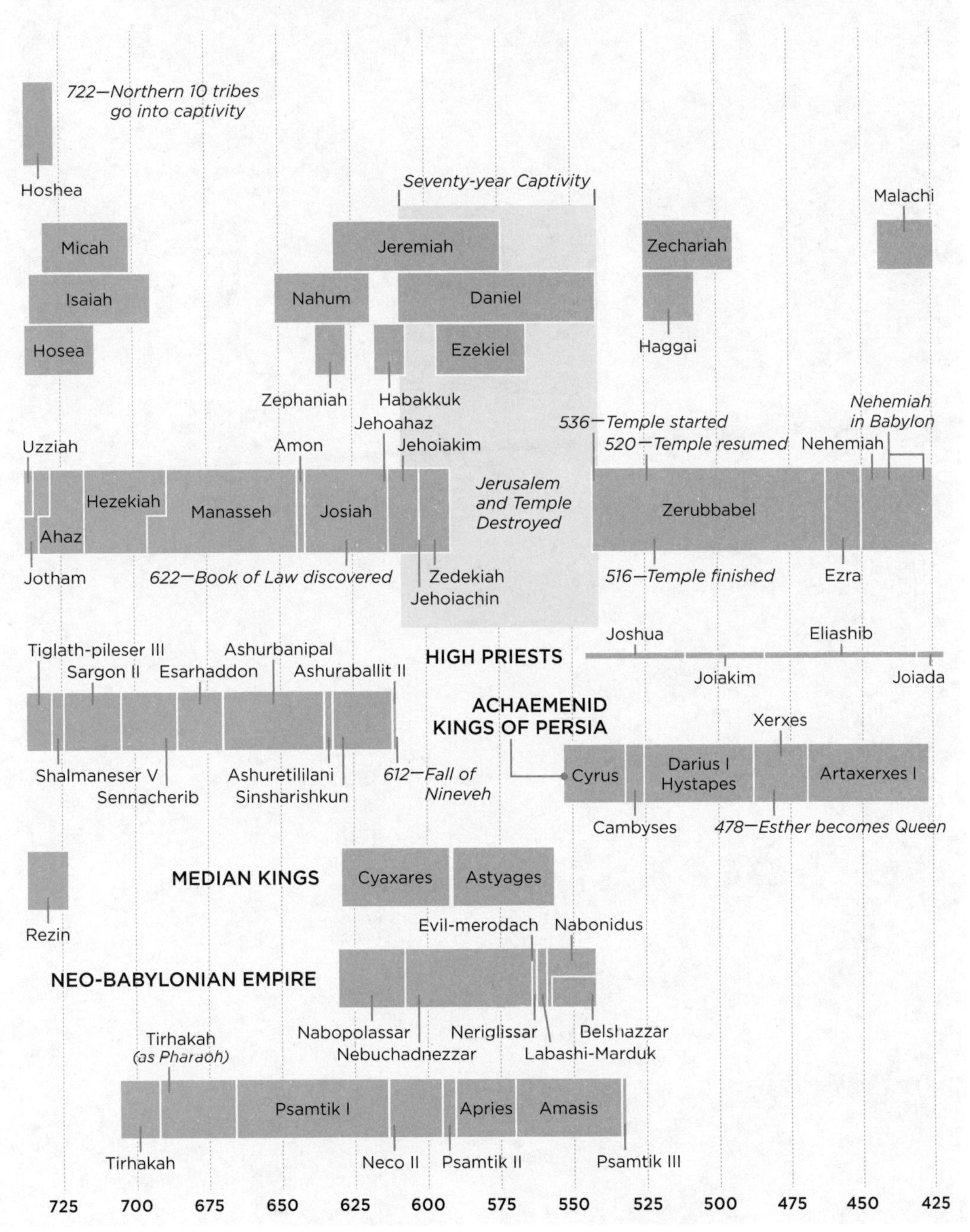

HELPFUL RESOURCES FOR STUDYING JONAH

Boice, James Montgomery. *The Minor Prophets: Two Volumes Complete in One Edition*. Grand Rapids, MI: Kregel, 1996.

Estelle, Bryan D. *Salvation through Judgment and Mercy: The Gospel according to Jonah*. The Gospel according to the Old Testament. Edited by Iain M. Duguid. Phillipsburg, NJ: P&R, 2005.

Ferguson, Sinclair. *Man Overboard!: The Story of Jonah*. Edinburgh: Banner of Truth, 1981.

Phillips, Richard D. *Jonah and Micah*. Reformed Expository Commentary. Edited by Richard D. Phillips and Philip G. Ryken. Phillipsburg, NJ: P&R, 2010.

Redmond, Eric C., Bill Curtis, and Ken Fentress. *Exalting Jesus in Jonah, Micah, Nahum, and Habakkuk*. Christ-Centered Exposition Commentary. Edited by David Platt et al. Nashville, TN: B&H, 2016.

NOTES

1. "The Setting of Jonah," map from page 1685 of the ESV® Study Bible (The Holy Bible, English Standard Version®), copyright © 2008 by Crossway, a publishing ministry of Good News Publishers. Used by permission. All rights reserved.
2. "Spokesmen for God: Exodus 7:1–7," Ligonier, January 1, 2013, https://www.ligonier.org.
3. ESV Study Bible (Wheaton, IL: Crossway, 2008), note on Jonah 1:1.
4. "Did You Know?" in ESV Student Study Bible (Wheaton, IL: Crossway, 2011), 602.
5. James Montgomery Boice, *The Minor Prophets: Two Volumes Complete in One Edition* (Grand Rapids, MI: Kregel, 1996), 217.
6. Richard D. Phillips, *Jonah and Micah*, Reformed Expository Commentary, ed. Richard D. Phillips and Philip G. Ryken (Phillipsburg, NJ: P&R, 2010), 29–30.
7. Phillips, *Jonah and Micah*, 31.
8. Phillips, *Jonah and Micah*, 60.
9. Jacques Ellul, cited in Bryan D. Estelle, *Salvation through Judgment and Mercy: The Gospel according to Jonah*, The Gospel according to the Old Testament, ed. Iain M. Duguid (Phillipsburg, NJ: P&R, 2005), 59–60.
10. John Currid, "Introduction to Leviticus," in ESV Study Bible, 211–16.
11. Phillips, *Jonah and Micah*, 59.
12. R. C. Sproul, "What Do Expiation and Propitiation Mean?," Ligonier, April 8, 2020, https://www.ligonier.org, emphasis added.
13. Phillips, *Jonah and Micah*, 67.
14. "Did You Know?" in ESV Student Study Bible, 654.
15. Phillips, *Jonah and Micah*, 75.
16. Ora Rowan, "Hast Thou Heard Him, Seen Him, Known Him," https://www.hymnal.net.
17. David Powlison, "Idols of the Heart and 'Vanity Fair,'" CCEF, October 16, 2009, https://www.ccef.org.
18. Boice, *The Minor Prophets*, 237.

19. Steven Lawson, "Is It Necessary to Preach Divine Wrath?," Ligonier, April 23, 2018, https://www.ligonier.org.
20. Phillips, *Jonah and Micah*, 102.
21. ESV Study Bible, note on Jonah 3:7–8.
22. Phillips, *Jonah and Micah*, 109.
23. Barry Cooper, "Immutability," Ligonier, December 7, 2021, https://www.ligonier.org.
24. Hugh Martin, cited in Phillips, *Jonah and Micah*, 110–11.
25. Boice, *The Minor Prophets*, 245.
26. Sinclair Ferguson, *Man Overboard!: The Story of Jonah* (Edinburgh: Banner of Truth, 1981), 83.
27. Dennis Baly, *The Geography of the Bible* (London: Lutherworth, 1957), 67–68.
28. Peter Williams, cited in Phillips, *Jonah and Micah*, 123–24.
29. "Chronology of Old Testament Kings and Prophets" table, taken from pages 10–11 of The MacArthur Study Bible, English Standard Version®, copyright 2010 by Crossway. Used by permission. All rights reserved.

Flourish Bible Study Series